WATER

noun
An odorless, tasteless liquid that falls from the clouds as precipitation to form streams, lakes, rivers, and seas; covers 70% of Earth; freezes at 32°F and boils at 212°F; is a major part of all living things.

Doe Boyle

illustrated by
Ana Miminoshvili

Albert Whitman & Company
Chicago, Illinois

In the peace of early morning, a dewdrop forms in a meadow.

And another and another—until every blade of grass, every leaf of clover, sparkles as thousands of tiny water droplets in the air turn from gas to liquid.

Like crystal beads, the dewdrops glisten— and when we walk through the meadow, they burst. Their cool water soaks our toes.

All of the water on Earth today has been here for billions of years. Every drop. Everything that lives on Earth needs water to survive.

In moments like this one, it is easy to see that water is everywhere. And that is good because, without water, there can be no life on Earth as we know it. All these waterdrops are essential for life.

Water is the most common
substance on Earth's surface.
And it is always in motion.

All those zillions of drops of water,
rushing and rambling in our brooks,
streams, and rivers.

All those zillions of drops of water,
rolling and tumbling in our oceans.

Drops of water in the air we breathe.
Drops of water in the food we eat.

And drops cycling through the cells
of every single organism—every plant,
every creature, every human—that
has ever lived.

Earth formed about 4.5 billion years ago, but it had no water on its surface—not one drop—until about 4.3 billion years ago. Life may have begun in Earth's oceans about 3.5 billion years ago. Every organism that has ever existed on Earth began in its oceans. All life is connected to water—even though some organisms moved onto the land.

Water covers about 70% of our planet. It helps divide, shape, and connect our seven continents.

Many ocean species have not been identified because so much of the world's oceans has not yet been explored.

Each of those drops of water is a shape-shifter.
Water is the only substance on Earth that
exists naturally in three different forms.
Water can be a liquid, a solid, or a gas.

When water is a liquid,
its droplets move freely.
They gush and seep.
They drizzle and puddle.
They pour and pool.

When water is a solid, it is hard. The waterdrops are frozen.
Solid water may be a glacier, an iceberg, an icicle—
or it may be a crystal of six-sided snow.
It may be a bouncing ball of hail that lasts just a minute—
or a sleek pellet of sleet that melts in a second.

When water is a gas, or vapor, the drops are invisible. Water vapor is made of
water droplets so tiny that they float in the air. Even though we cannot see these
droplets, they are always in the air around us.

In all of these forms—liquid, solid, and gas—each of these waterdrops on Earth
is reused and recycled. In each of these three forms, water is in constant motion,
reaching the organisms that cannot exist without it.

In movements we may see, in movements we may hardly notice, and in movements
that are invisible, water is always changing—all around us, every day.

The movement of water droplets is part of a process called the water cycle. About 4.3 billion years ago, hot water vapor escaped from Earth's core through cracks in its crust.

The vapor rose into Earth's cool atmosphere, and Earth's gravity kept the water vapor from going into outer space. Heat from the sun helped create a never-ending cycle of melting ice, rising vapor, falling rain, and flowing water. From that time onward, all those waterdrops created the endless motion we still have today.

This water droplet cycle goes around and around, without end, connecting all of Earth's water. All life on Earth depends on water's continual movement and its changes from one form to another.

We may not see the water vapor around and above us, but we often see clouds in the sky.

Clouds are made of liquid water droplets or ice crystals so small that they float in the atmosphere. The cloud droplets do not fall until they grow larger and heavier, forming rain, which returns to the ground as liquid. This water, falling from the clouds, is called precipitation.

Less than 1% of Earth's water is in the vapor in its atmosphere. If the water vapor floating in the atmosphere were to fall as rain all at the same time, Earth would be covered in an extra inch of water.

When cloud droplets get both heavier and colder, they may freeze into solid crystals of snow or hail, which also fall to the ground. Fog and mist also return to the ground as liquid.

All these forms of precipitation are important in the water cycle because they are the ways that water returns to Earth's surface from the atmosphere.

We need clouds to make rain and protect us from the sun's heat. Every day, more than half the earth is covered in clouds.

When the hot water vapor
escaped from Earth's core
4.3 billion years ago, the oceans
that formed as Earth cooled were made of
fresh water, with very little or no salt. Today,
water that falls as rain is also fresh water.
Humans can drink fresh water.

The water in our oceans became salty when all those raindrops wore away salts in the rocks on land, carrying the salts into Earth's rivers and streams—and then onward to the oceans. Ocean water today is salt water. Humans cannot drink salt water.

Hot rocks deep in Earth's core released salts that worked their way through Earth's crust and were also added to the seawater.

If all the salt in the oceans were collected, dried, and spread out evenly on the surfaces of Earth's continents, it would form a layer more than 500 feet thick—as tall as a building forty floors high.

Earth's oceans contain more than 97% of our water—and we cannot drink it.

Wetlands absorb harmful chemicals, and they help hold sand and soil in place along coasts. They exist on every continent except Antarctica.

Most of Earth's falling drops of water land in our vast oceans. Falling freshwater drops also collect in lakes, ponds, puddles, and reservoirs. Some drops settle into swamps, bogs, and marshes that stay moist, sometimes all year. These wetlands act like sponges, soaking up rainwater that might otherwise cause flooding.

Full of plant life, wetlands give homes to reptiles, fish, frogs, and other amphibians. They are safe places for migrating birds to rest.

Some waterdrops sink into the soil. This water is called groundwater. It supplies water to farms to irrigate fields and to factories to run machinery.

Pockets of space under the ground can hold water for days or for hundreds of years.

In places where other freshwater sources are scarce, groundwater can save lives. Humans also dig wells to reach groundwater.

Even though countless drops of water are recycled every day, almost one billion people on Earth do not have access to clean, safe water. Our warming planet can lead to changes that cause extreme weather.

In deserts, where rain is rare, people struggle to find food because grasses and grains cannot grow in parched soil. People may have to walk hours to find water.

People invent ways to find and protect every drop of water. They dig deep underground wells and pump water to the surface. They plant new seeds, drizzling them with the found groundwater.

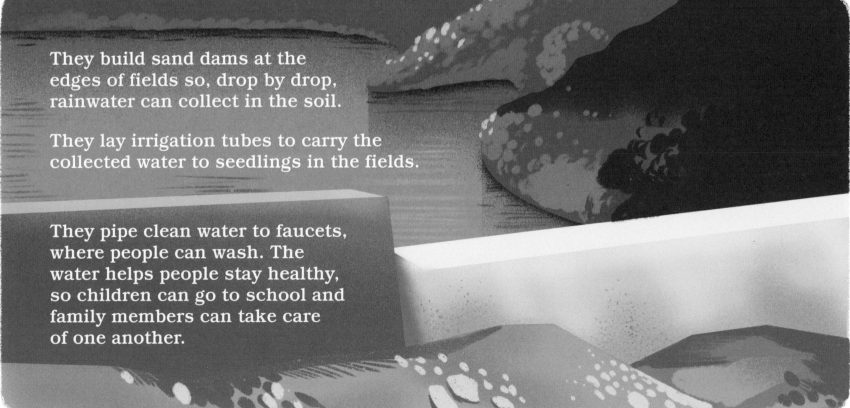

They build sand dams at the edges of fields so, drop by drop, rainwater can collect in the soil.

They lay irrigation tubes to carry the collected water to seedlings in the fields.

They pipe clean water to faucets, where people can wash. The water helps people stay healthy, so children can go to school and family members can take care of one another.

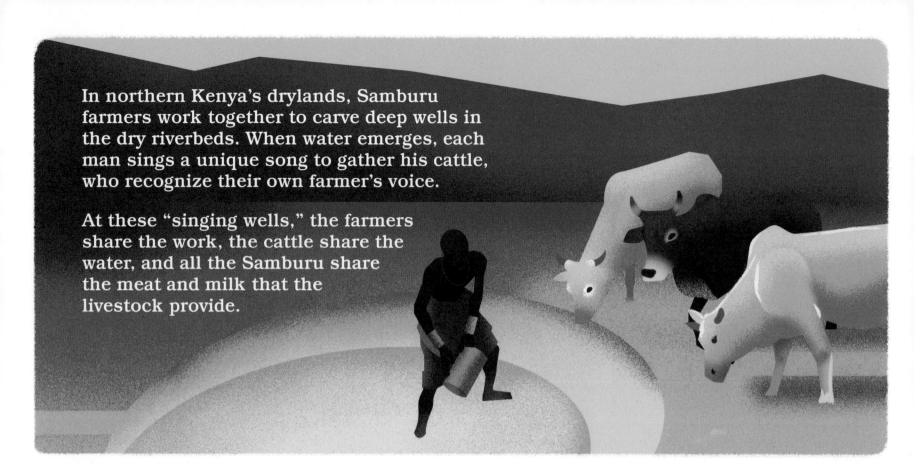

In northern Kenya's drylands, Samburu farmers work together to carve deep wells in the dry riverbeds. When water emerges, each man sings a unique song to gather his cattle, who recognize their own farmer's voice.

At these "singing wells," the farmers share the work, the cattle share the water, and all the Samburu share the meat and milk that the livestock provide.

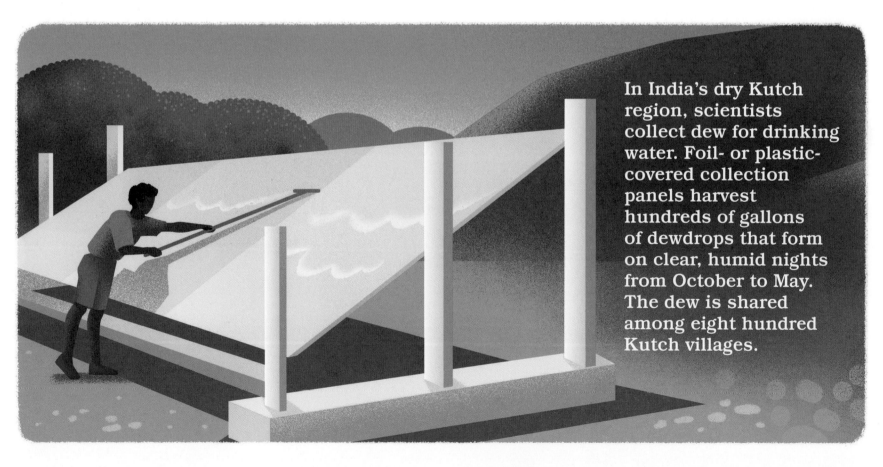

In India's dry Kutch region, scientists collect dew for drinking water. Foil- or plastic-covered collection panels harvest hundreds of gallons of dewdrops that form on clear, humid nights from October to May. The dew is shared among eight hundred Kutch villages.

Rainfall is rare in Bellavista, Peru. But from June to November huge banks of dense fog from the Pacific Ocean blow across the village. People build plastic-mesh nets called fog catchers. When the fog rolls in, each net can catch up to 150 gallons of water droplets in one day. Gutters and tubes carry the water to storage tanks and to a community vegetable garden.

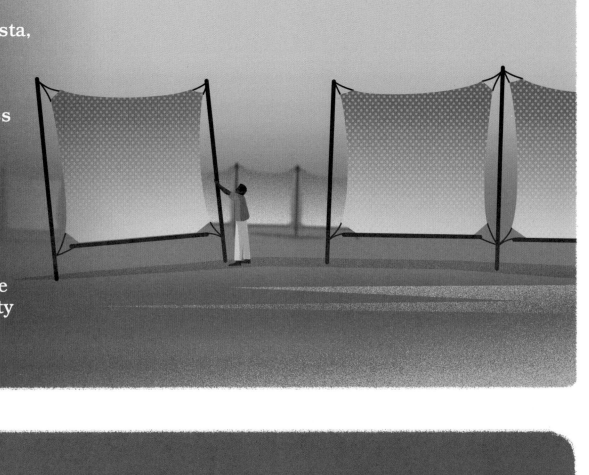

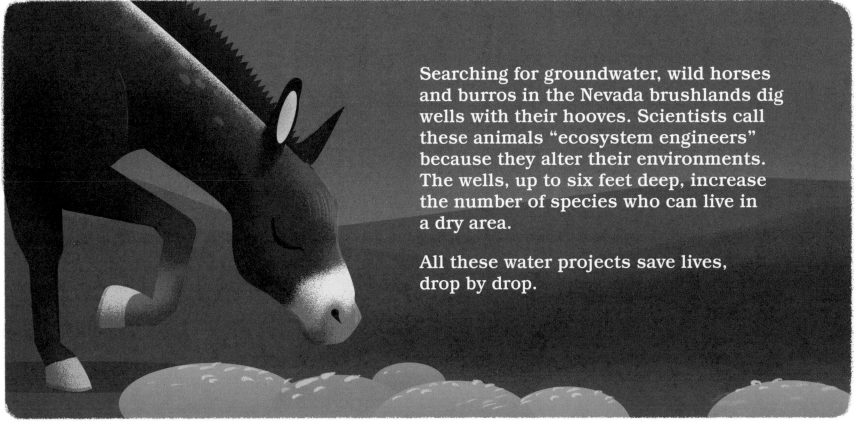

Searching for groundwater, wild horses and burros in the Nevada brushlands dig wells with their hooves. Scientists call these animals "ecosystem engineers" because they alter their environments. The wells, up to six feet deep, increase the number of species who can live in a dry area.

All these water projects save lives, drop by drop.

The waterdrops also help plants grow.

Water carries food from the soil to a plant, through the plant's roots, and through the whole plant.

Plants catch waterdrops in their leaves too.

Water helps plants stay sturdy, supporting stems, leaves, branches, and flowers.

Water helps plants form fruit, make pollen and nectar, and produce seeds for new plants.

And plants make a difference to every living being.

Plants use water, along with air and sunlight, to make their food. This process is called photosynthesis.

Water helps keeps plants at temperatures that allow them to grow, bloom, and make food we can eat. If a plant becomes too hot or if it has extra water, it releases the water in the form of vapor through small pores on the undersides of its leaves.

This is called transpiration, and it happens every day in millions of plants, including trees. All the trees in one forest create an enormous current of tiny, invisible water droplets in the air. These droplets, carried by wind, form clouds that make rain, which may drop right back onto the forest or fall hundreds or thousands of miles away.

The amount of water that enters the air from plants and trees changes every day—but every drop counts.

One large, leafy tree in a forest can release 40,000 gallons of water into the air each year.

The same drops of water also cycle through all living beings. Every process that happens inside every part of humans and animals relies on the water they drink. Nothing works well—or for long—without water.

Water carries dissolved nutrients through our bodies, feeding us, giving us energy, and keeping us healthy. Water's speedy delivery system helps every living being grow and stay strong.

People are made up of about 60 percent water—mostly stored in our muscles. Every drop helps our muscles keep their strength. But those drops do more.

Water helps humans—and animals—breathe easily by thinning the coating of mucus that lines our air passages and lungs.

Water cushions our joints and helps keep us flexible so we can move more easily.

Without water, our joints would become sore, and our movements would stiffen.

All those drops of water also act as a shock absorber for the spinal cord, keeping bones from rubbing against each other.

In humans and most animals, water carries waste out of the body through pee, breath, and sweat.

Water helps all living beings keep their
bodies at just the right temperatures by
releasing heat through breath and sweat.

When we breathe in, moist air travels through
our bodies, picking up heat. When we exhale, warm
breath leaves our bodies as water vapor. These releases
of heat help keep our temperatures steady.

When we sweat, water leaves our bodies as liquid through pores in our skin. The outside air makes the sweat evaporate, or change from a liquid to a vapor. As the sweat turns into vapor, we cool down.

Every drop of water in the bodies of living beings protects them and helps keep them comfortable.

Humans and animals can survive without water for only a few days. Without water, we cannot sweat, so we can't adjust our body temperature. Without water, we cannot breathe or swallow easily.

Sometimes, water simply comforts us.
It helps keep our bodies, homes, and clothes clean.
It helps heal our scuffs and scrapes.
We can listen to the gurgle of a brook,
the roar of a waterfall,
and the rise and fall of a shifting tide,
or we can watch the rolling waves.

But water is not limitless.

Water that is plentiful in one place cannot be easily shared with people who need water in another place. Our water supply is not endless, and it is not evenly spread out across Earth.

Sixty percent of Earth's fresh water is found in just nine countries: Brazil, Canada, China, Colombia, the Democratic Republic of Congo, India, Indonesia, Russia, and the United States. The United States uses the most drinkable water each year; each person uses about 80 to 150 gallons of water each day. In the Democratic Republic of Congo, each person uses about 31 gallons per day.

When water is hard to find, most living organisms suffer. Without water, all the life processes of plants and animals slow—and then stop. To preserve life, we must have water.

Drop by drop, each of us can help make sure
there is enough water for everyone.

We can catch and conserve water, capturing
rainwater in buckets or barrels and dribbling the
raindrops into our gardens.

We can turn off faucets while we brush our teeth
and wash our dishes.

We can take quick showers.

We can help conserve some of Earth's water for
someone else, somewhere else.

Every person makes a difference.

Every drop makes a difference.

We can help preserve water around the world,
one drop at a time.

Author's Note

As I wrote this book, researching water facts and remembering the water science I learned as a child, I rediscovered the enormous role that water plays on Earth. As a child, I saw that water shapes the landscape and creates places of beauty. Over time, I understood that water is both powerful and precious. It brings life to all plants and all creatures—and no living organism can survive without it.

I hope all readers will discover water's importance to our bodies, the significance of its presence on Earth, and its meaning to everything that lives. In all of the solar system— in fact, in all of the universe—Earth is the only place we know where liquid surface water has made life possible. And humans may be the only living beings who can take an active role in protecting it and conserving it.

In our own habitats—in our homes and neighborhoods—each one of us can be a community caretaker. We can help keep our nearest waterways and bodies of water clean, and we can reduce our personal use of water to help ensure that enough remains for the survival of others. If we are careful stewards of water, then the same droplets that may have refreshed the dinosaurs will flow onward through us toward everyone ahead.

Resources

books for children

Bang, Molly, and Penny Chisholm. *Rivers of Sunlight: How the Sun Moves Water around the Earth*. New York: Blue Sky, 2017.

Kerley, Barbara. *A Cool Drink of Water*. Washington, DC: National Geographic, 2002.

Lyon, George Ella, and Katherine Tillotson. *All the Water in the World*. New York: Atheneum, 2011.

Paul, Miranda. *Water Is Water: A Book about the Water Cycle*. New York: Roaring Brook, 2015.

Sayre, April Pulley. *Raindrops Roll*. New York: Beach Lane, 2015.

Simon, Seymour. *Oceans*. New York: Collins, 2006.

Stewart, Melissa. *Water*. Washington, DC: National Geographic, 2014.

Strauss, Rochelle. *One Well: The Story of Water on Earth*. Toronto: Kids Can, 2007.

Wells, Robert E. *Did a Dinosaur Drink This Water?* Morton Grove, IL: Albert Whitman, 2006.

Wick, Walter. *A Drop of Water: A Book of Science and Wonder*. New York: Scholastic, 1997.

Glossary

atmosphere: the layer of gas, often called air, that surrounds Earth and is held in place by gravity.

cell: the smallest unit of living matter able to function independently.

cold-blooded: an animal whose body temperatures is regulated by its environment.

continent: one of the seven great land masses on Earth; Africa, Antarctica, Asia, Australia, Europe, North America, and South America.

dewdrop: a droplet of water that condenses from the air, often overnight, onto a cool surface.

Earth's core: the hot, dense, ball-shaped center of planet Earth.

gas: a basic form of matter that has no fixed shape and tends to expand without limit, or to the shape of whatever space is available.

gravity: an invisible force that pulls, or attracts, objects toward each other or makes objects or substances fall toward the surface of Earth.

habitat: a place in nature where an animal or plant normally lives or grows.

hail: a type of precipitation that forms when drops of water in thunderstorm clouds freeze and fall to the ground as frozen pellets.

liquid: a basic form of matter that is neither a solid nor a gas and can move freely within the shape of any container in which it is placed.

mucus: the slippery, sticky coating that moistens and protects body membranes such as noses, throats, and lungs.

organism: a living body made up of parts that work together to carry on the processes of life.

pollen: the fine, powdery grains in flowers.

pores: tiny openings such as in skin or on a leaf's surface through which liquids or gases may pass.

reptiles: cold-blooded animals, such as snakes, turtles, and crocodiles, that have a backbone, are covered with scales or horny plates, and breathe through lungs.

sleet: a type of precipitation that forms when falling snow melts and then quickly freezes again before it touches the ground.

spinal cord: the long bundle of nerve fibers and tissue that runs from the base of the skull through the backbone, or spine, and forms the main pathway for messages between the brain and nearly all parts of the body.

tissue: a mass of cells or a layer of cells that forms the basic structure of all plant or animal bodies and work together to do a job in the body.

universe: all of space and everything in it, including its energy and matter.

vapor: a substance in the air in the basic form of matter called gas.